DRUM RH... SPELLER

by HAROLD M. SHLIMOVITZ

A SYSTEMATIZED SET OF WORK SHEETS FOR SUPPLEMENTING ANY ELEMENTARY CLASS OR PRIVATE METHOD.

DESIGNED TO HELP THE STUDENT GAIN A BETTER UNDERSTANDING OF THE PROBLEMS OF FINGERING AND READING MUSIC AND AT THE SAME TIME SAVE VALUABLE LESSON TIME.

ESSENTIAL SNARE DRUM RUDIMENTS

(This page should be used for individual practice and reference)

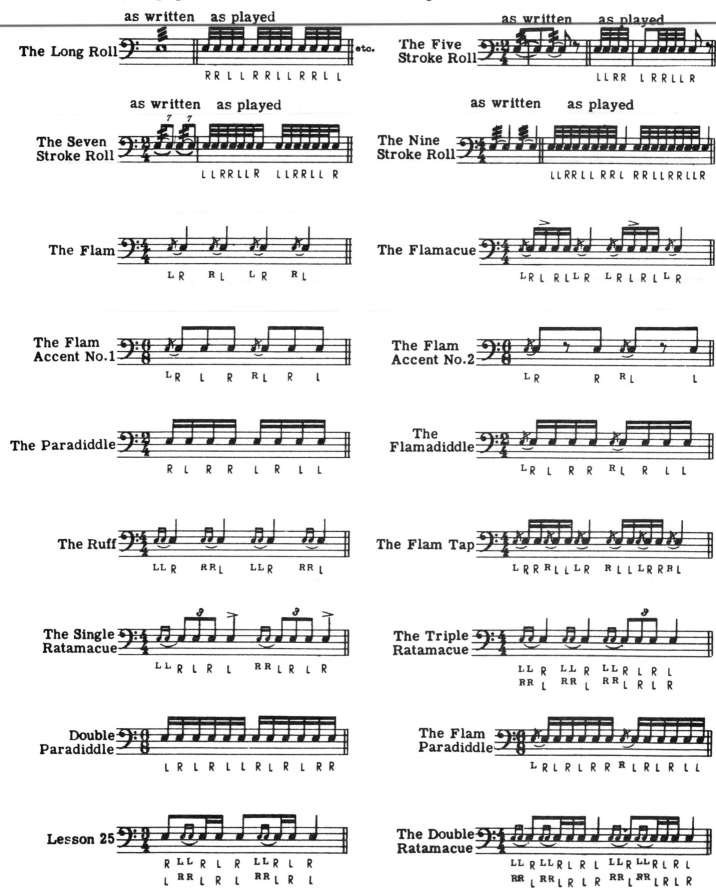

LESSON 1

You should know the following.

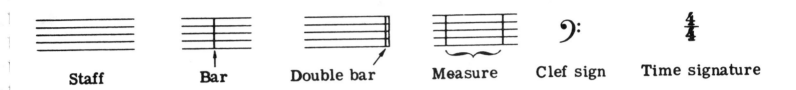

Staff   Bar   Double bar   Measure   Clef sign   Time signature

1   Match the symbols in the **TOP** line with their names.
The first one is done for you.

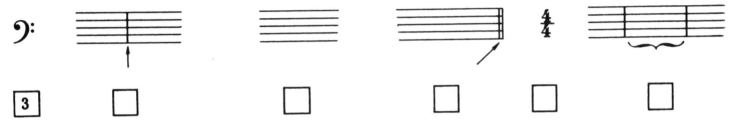

1-Staff; 2-Measure; 3-Clef sign; 4-Bar; 5-Time signature; 6-Double bar.

2   The Bass Clef sign (𝄢) is usually found at the beginning of each staff of Drum music.
There are 4 easy steps in learning to draw this sign.

a - Step 1 - Place a large dot on the 4th line.

Step 2-Make a curved line touching the top line of the staff.

Step 3-Continue the curved line down to the 2nd line.

Step 4-Put two dots after it, one on each side of the 4th line.

b - Draw 3 dots as in step 1 above.

Draw 3 curved lines touching the top line as in step 2 above.

Continue the curved line as in step 3 above and add the 2 dots as in step 4.

Draw 3 complete Bass Clef signs.

LESSON 2

1   Place the count under the note - <u>use</u> <u>x</u> <u>for</u> <u>rests.</u>

1 2 3 4   1 2 3 x

LESSON 3

1 Write in notes to match numbers listed below.   Rests to match x.

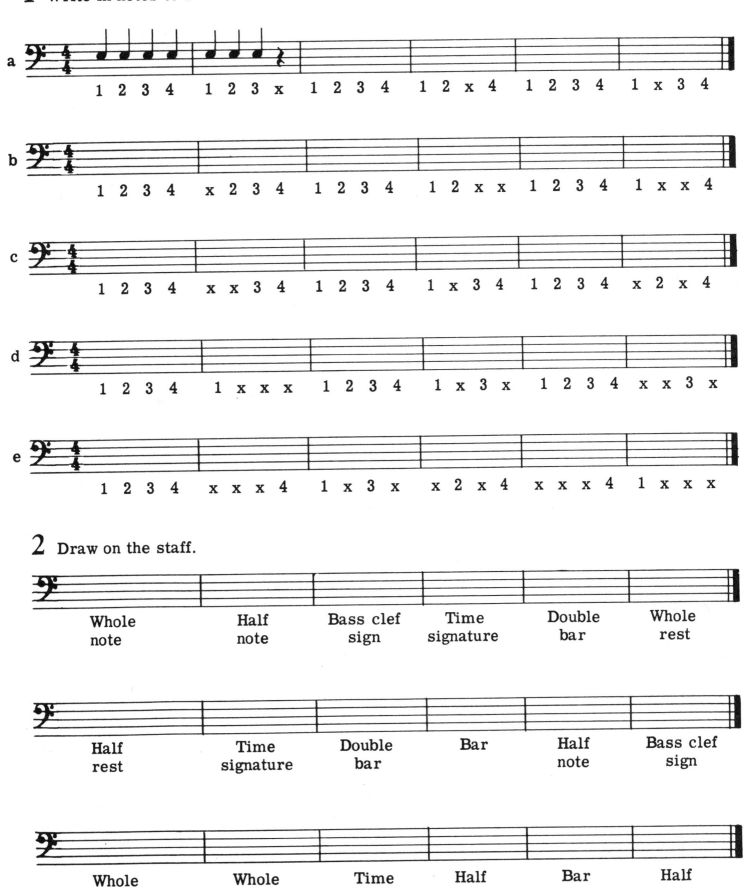

2 Draw on the staff.

| Whole note | Half note | Bass clef sign | Time signature | Double bar | Whole rest |

| Half rest | Time signature | Double bar | Bar | Half note | Bass clef sign |

| Whole rest | Whole note | Time signature | Half rest | Bar | Half note |

LESSON 4

1 Place the sticking below the notes. Use x for rests.
*Alternate the sticking.

a

```
L  R  L  R   L  R  L  x
*R  L  R  L   R  L  R  x
```

b

c

d

e

2 PREPARATION FOR THE LONG ROLL
Place the sticking below the notes as indicated.
*Alternate the sticking.

a

```
L  L  R  R
*R  R  L  L
```

Place notes for the sticking indicated below.

b

```
L L R R    L L R R    L L R R    L L R R    L L R R
```

EL. 1063

LESSON 5

1 Place the count under the notes. Use x for rests.

a

1 + 2 + 3 + 4 +   1 + 2 + 3 + 4 x

b

c

d

2 PREPARATION FOR THE 5 - STROKE ROLL.
   a. Place the sticking below the notes as indicated. Use x for rests.
    *Alternate sticking.

L L R R L   x
*R R L L R   x

   b. Place notes on the staff to match the sticking indicated below.

L L R R L   L L R R L   L L R R L   L L R R L

LESSON 6

Eighth Notes

We have had drill using 4 kinds of notes and rests.

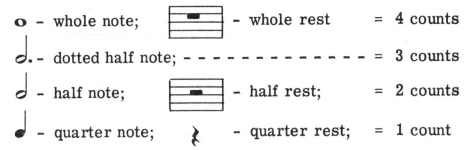

o - whole note;	▭ - whole rest	= 4 counts
𝅘𝅥. - dotted half note; - - - - - - - - - - - -		= 3 counts
𝅗𝅥 - half note;	▭ - half rest;	= 2 counts
𝅘𝅥 - quarter note;	𝄽 - quarter rest;	= 1 count

From now on our work will include eighth notes.   The eighth note gets only one half count and it takes two of them to make one count. In other words, two eighth notes are played on one count.

A single eighth note looks like this - ♪
When we have two together on one
count they are joined like this   - ♫
This is an eighth rest   - 𝄾

1   In the measures below, on what count do we play the eighth notes?

_____   _____   _____   _____ & _____   _____ & _____

2   Put in the Bars and write counts.

3   a - Complete the Time signature.
     b - Write counting under each measure.

LESSON 7

1 Write in notes to match the count below. Write in rests for x.

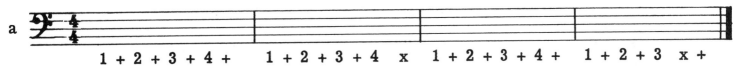

a

1 + 2 + 3 + 4 +   1 + 2 + 3 + 4 x   1 + 2 + 3 + 4 +   1 + 2 + 3 x +

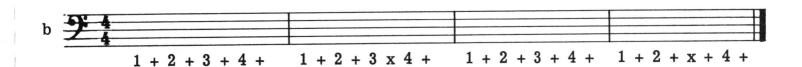

b

1 + 2 + 3 + 4 +   1 + 2 + 3 x 4 +   1 + 2 + 3 + 4 +   1 + 2 + x + 4 +

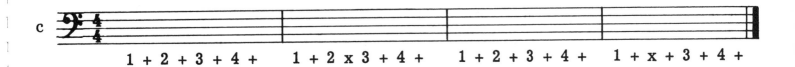

c

1 + 2 + 3 + 4 +   1 + 2 x 3 + 4 +   1 + 2 + 3 + 4 +   1 + x + 3 + 4 +

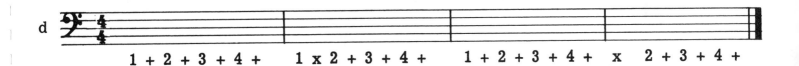

d

1 + 2 + 3 + 4 +   1 x 2 + 3 + 4 +   1 + 2 + 3 + 4 + x   2 + 3 + 4 +

2 a – Match the Notes on the staff with the rest, or rests, receiving the same number of counts.

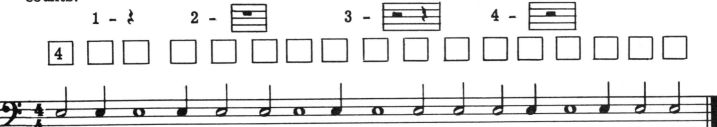

b – Match the Rests on the staff with the note receiving the same number of counts. (In 4/4 time).

LESSON 8

1 Match the Symbols on the staff with their names.
The first one is done for you.

1 – Sharp	5 – Clef Sign	9 – Half note
2 – Tie	6 – Whole Note	10 – Flat
3 – Bar	7 – Quarter rest	11 – Quarter note
4 – Time Signature	8 – Natural sign	12 – Half rest
		13 – Whole rest

2 Give the number of counts the notes and rests receive in 4/4 time.

3 Write the counting in the measures below. The first measure is done for you.
Always remember to think the number of the count when playing.

1 2 3 4

LESSON 9

1 Place the sticking below notes. Use x for the rests.
Alternate the sticking.

2 PREPARATION FOR THE 7-STROKE ROLL
a. Place the sticking below the notes as indicated.

L L R R L L R

b. Place notes on the staff to match the sticking.

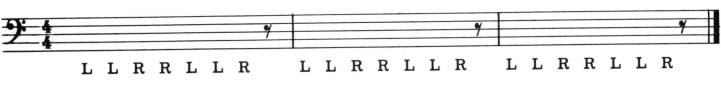

L L R R L L R   L L R R L L R   L L R R L L R

LESSON 10

1 Place the count under the note.   Use x for rest.

a

1 + 2 + 3 + 4 +   1 + 2 + 3 + x x

b

c

2 PREPARATION FOR THE 9 - STROKE ROLL
a. Place sticking below the note as indicated.   *Alternate sticking.

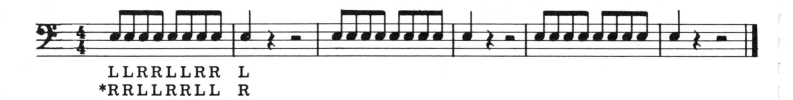

L L R R L L R R   L
*R R L L R R L L   R

3 Write the counting under the following measures.

1 2 3 4

EL. 1063

LESSON 11

1 Write in correct notes and rests to match the count below.
Write in the rests for x.

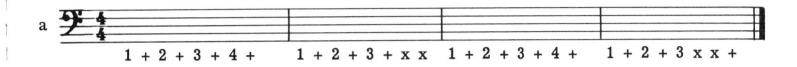

a

1 + 2 + 3 + 4 +   1 + 2 + 3 + x x   1 + 2 + 3 + 4 +   1 + 2 + 3 x x +

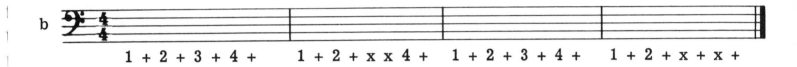

b

1 + 2 + 3 + 4 +   1 + 2 + x x 4 +   1 + 2 + 3 + 4 +   1 + 2 + x + x +

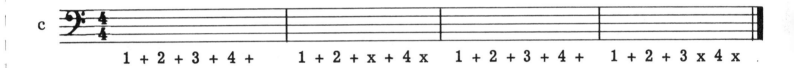

c

1 + 2 + 3 + 4 +   1 + 2 + x + 4 x   1 + 2 + 3 + 4 +   1 + 2 + 3 x 4 x

2 LONG ROLL PREPARATION REVIEW.
Put the sticking below as indicated.   *Alternate the sticking.

L   L   R   R
*R   R   L   L

3 Write the note receiving the number of counts called for in 4/4 time.

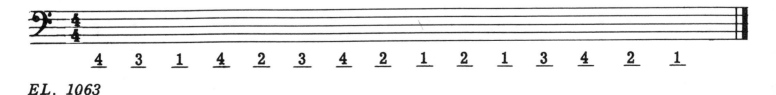

4   3   1   4   2   3   4   2   1   2   1   3   4   2   1

LESSON 12

1 Place the count under the notes.   Use x for rests.

2 Three of the most common kinds of time are 4/4; 3/4, & 2/4.
4/4 means there are 4 counts in each measure.
3/4 means there are 3 counts in each measure.
2/4 means there are 2 counts in each measure.

Put the correct time signature at the beginning of each measure.

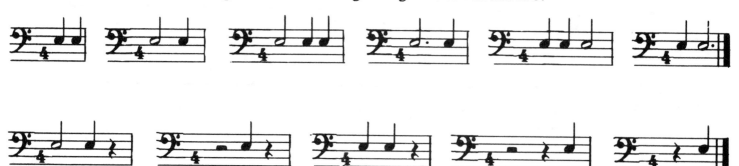

3 Write the counting under the measures below.

LESSON 13

1 Place the correct count under the notes. Use x for rests.

1 + 2 + 3

2 Add the time received by the notes, in 4/4 time, and put the total in the square.

o + 𝅗𝅥 + 𝅘𝅥 = ☐		o + 𝅗𝅥 + o = ☐
𝅘𝅥 + 𝅗𝅥 + 𝅘𝅥 = ☐		𝅗𝅥 + 𝅗𝅥 + 𝅘𝅥 = ☐
o + 𝅗𝅥 + 𝅗𝅥 = ☐		𝅘𝅥 + 𝅘𝅥 + 𝅗𝅥 = ☐
𝅘𝅥 + o + 𝅗𝅥 = ☐		𝅗𝅥 + 𝅗𝅥 + 𝅗𝅥 = ☐
𝅘𝅥 + 𝅗𝅥 + 𝅗𝅥 = ☐		𝅗𝅥 + o + 𝅘𝅥 = ☐

3 Match the following.

D . C.   - ☐   1 - The end

Fine   - ☐   2 - Repeat

▦   - ☐   3 - Go back to the beginning

𝄐   - ☐   4 - 4/4 time

c   - ☐   5 - Give extra time (hold).

EL. 1063

LESSON 14

1 Write in quarter notes and rests to match the count below.   Use rests for x.

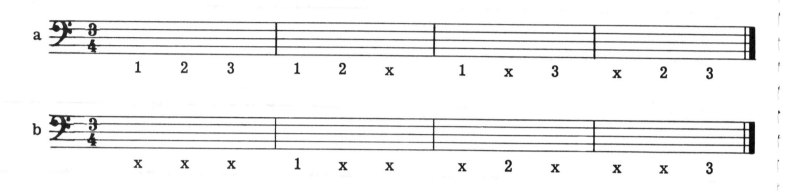

a

```
1   2   3   |   1   2   x   |   1   x   3   |   x   2   3
```

b

```
x   x   x   |   1   x   x   |   x   2   x   |   x   x   3
```

2 Write in eighth notes and eighth rests for the count below.   Use rests for x.

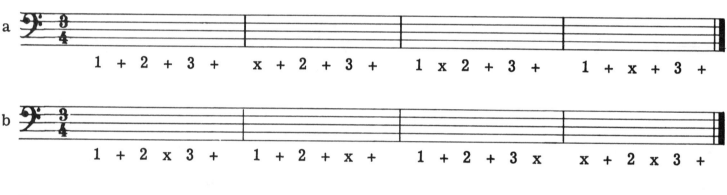

a

```
1 + 2 + 3 +   |   x + 2 + 3 +   |   1 x 2 + 3 +   |   1 + x + 3 +
```

b

```
1 + 2 x 3 +   |   1 + 2 + x +   |   1 + 2 + 3 x   |   x + 2 x 3 +
```

c

```
1 x 2 x 3 +   |   1 + x + x +   |   x + x + x +   |   1 x 2 x 3 x
```

d

```
x x 2 + 3 +   |   1 + x x 3 +   |   1 + 2 + x x   |   x x 2 x 3 x
```

3 On the top staff is a series of notes and rests. You are to rewrite this line on the bottom staff changing notes to rests of the same time value and rests to notes of the same time value.

sample   etc.

EL. 1063

LESSON 15

1 Write the count under the note.   Use x for the rest.

1 e + a 2   +

1   + a 2   +

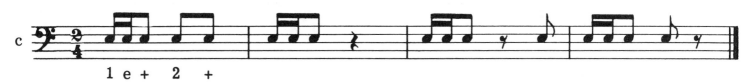

1 e +   2   +

2 PREPARATION FOR THE LONG ROLL (Review)
Write in the sticking as indicated.   *Alternate the sticking.

Note: The Long Roll is written:

3 PREPARATION FOR THE 5-STROKE ROLL (Review)
Write in the sticking as indicated.   *Alternate the sticking.

L   L   R   R   L
*R   R   L   L   R

Note: The 5-Stroke Roll is written: 2/4

LESSON 16

1 Write in the notes to correspond with the count below.
Use rests to correspond with the x.

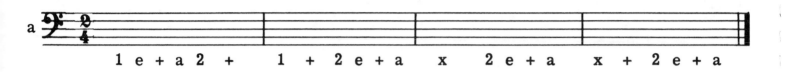

a   1 e + a 2 +   1 + 2 e + a x   2 e + a   x + 2 e + a

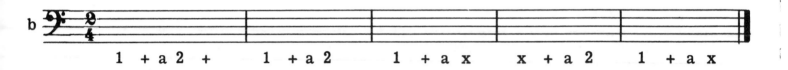

b   1 + a 2 +   1 + a 2   1 + a x   x + a 2   1 + a x

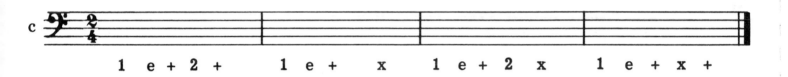

c   1 e + 2 +   1 e +   x   1 e + 2 x   1 e + x +

2 a – Put in the Bar lines. (Note Time Signatures).
b – Write the counting under each measure.

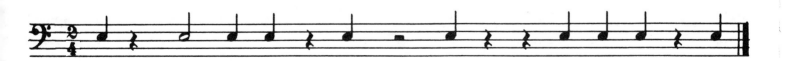

LESSON 17

1 Write in the sticking under the notes as indicated.
Alternate the sticking.

a

```
L R L R L R
R L R L R L
```

b

c

2 PREPARATION FOR THE 7-STROKE ROLL
Write in the sticking as indicated.

```
L   L   R   R   L   L   R   x
```

Note: The 7-Stroke Roll is written:

3 Put the following on the staff below:

1 - Sharp	6 - Natural sign
2 - Half note	7 - Flat
3 - Clef sign	8 - Whole rest
4 - Time signature	9 - Half rest
5 - Quarter rest	10 - Dotted Half note

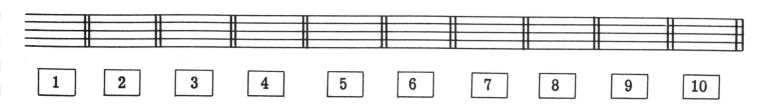

LESSON 18

1 PREPARATION FOR THE 9-STROKE ROLL
Write in sticking under the note as indicated.   *Alternate sticking.

L   L   R   R   R   L   L   R   R   L
*R   R   L   L   L   R   R   L   L   R

Note: The 9-Stroke
Roll is written:

2 PREPARATION FOR THE 13-STROKE ROLL
Write in sticking under the note as indicated.   *Alternate sticking.

L   L   R   R   L   L   R   R   L   L   R   R   L
*R   R   L   L   R   R   L   L   R   R   L   L   R

Note: The 13-Stroke
Roll is written:

3 Complete the Time Signatures.

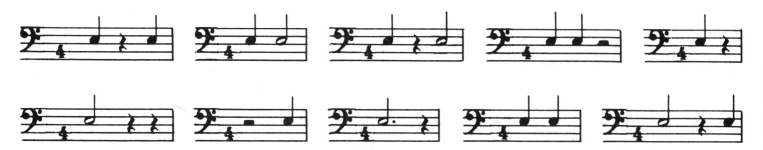

Put in Bar lines and write counting under each measure.

LESSON 19

1 Add the time of the notes and rests in 4/4 time.

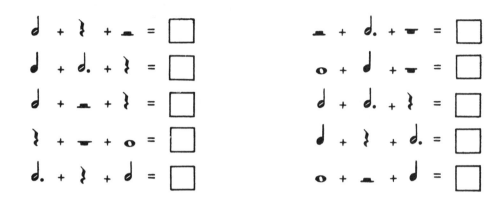

2 PREPARATION FOR THE PARADIDDLE
Write in the sticking as indicated.   *Alternate sticking.

```
 L    R    L    L
*R    L    R    R
```

3 PREPARATION FOR THE DOUBLE PARADIDDLE
Write in sticking as indicated below.   *Alternate sticking.

```
L R L R L L
R L R L R R
```

LESSON 20

1   Write the count under the note.   Use x for rests.

1 2 3 4 5 6

2   PREPARATION FOR THE RUFF
Write in the sticking as indicated.   *Alternate sticking.

L   L   R
*R   R   L

Note: The Ruff is written:

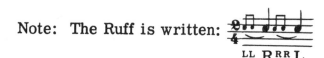

LL R RR L

3   On what count do the following examples start?

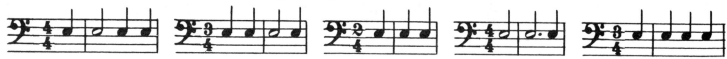

LESSON 21

1   Write in the notes to match the count below.
Rest to match the x.

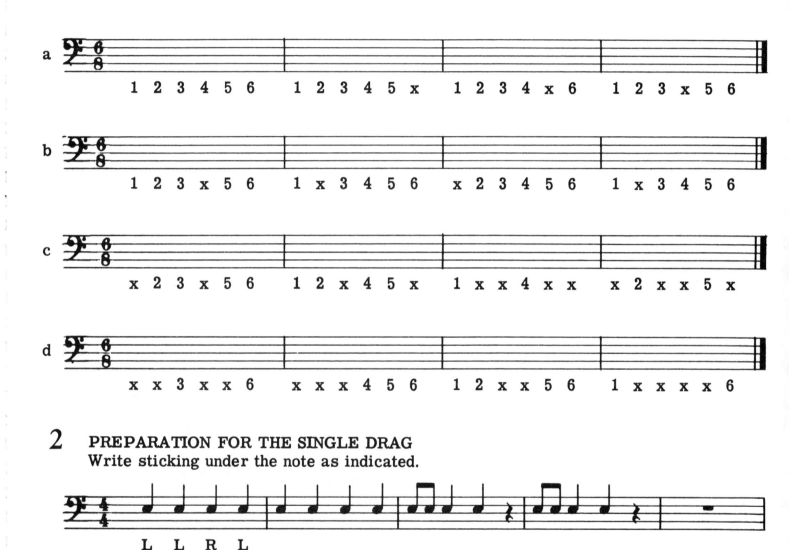

a
1 2 3 4 5 6   1 2 3 4 5 x   1 2 3 4 x 6   1 2 3 x 5 6

b
1 2 3 x 5 6   1 x 3 4 5 6   x 2 3 4 5 6   1 x 3 4 5 6

c
x 2 3 x 5 6   1 2 x 4 5 x   1 x x 4 x x   x 2 x x 5 x

d
x x 3 x x 6   x x x 4 5 6   1 2 x x 5 6   1 x x x x 6

2   **PREPARATION FOR THE SINGLE DRAG**
Write sticking under the note as indicated.

L L R L

L L R L L L R L

Note: The Single Drag is written:

LL R L

3   Add notes or rests to the measures below so each measure contains the correct number of counts.

LESSON 22

Write in the notes for the sticking of the following rudiments.

Long Roll.

LLRR   LLRR   LLRR   LLRR   LLRR   LLR   R

LLRR   LLRR   LLRR   LLRR   LLRR   LLRR

5-Stroke Roll.

LLRRL   LLRRL   LLRRL   LLRR

L   LLRRL   LLRRL   LLRRL   LLRRL

7-Stroke Roll.

LLRR   LLR   LLRR   LLR   LLRRLLR

LLRRLLR   LLRRLLR   LLRRLLR   LLRRLLR

9-Stroke Roll.

LLRR   LLRRL   LLRRLLRR   L   LLRRLLRR   L

LLRR   LLRR   L   LLRRLLRR   L

Ruff.

LLR   LLR   LLRLLR   LLRLLRLLRLLR

Single Drag.

LLRL   LLRL   LLRL   LLRL   LLRLLLRLLLRLLLRL

Paradiddle.

LRLL   LRLL   LRLLLRLL   LRLLLRLL

EL. 1063

LESSON 23

The Rudiments listed below are open and closed.   Match the open Rudiment with the number of the one which is closed.   The first one is done for you.

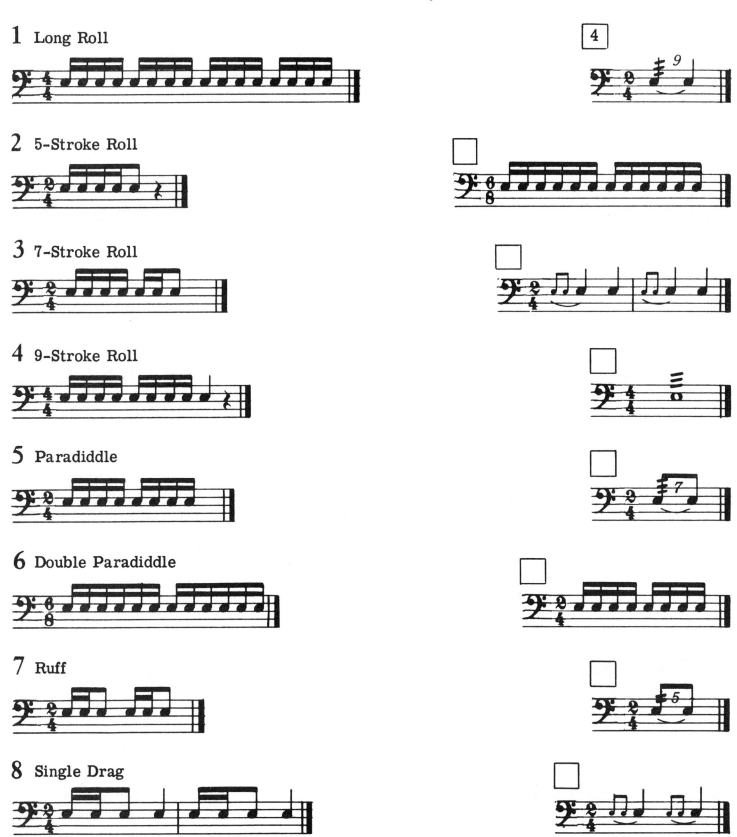

1 Long Roll

2 5-Stroke Roll

3 7-Stroke Roll

4 9-Stroke Roll

5 Paradiddle

6 Double Paradiddle

7 Ruff

8 Single Drag

LESSON 24

1 Join the stems on the notes below so you have the correct number of counts in each measure.

sample   etc.

2 Complete the measures below with either notes or rests.   (Note Time signature).

3 a - Put in measure bars.   (Note Time signature).
   b - Write counting under each measure.

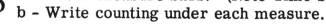

LESSON 25

Write in the sticking as indicated below.
Use a small letter for the Flam.

*Alternate the sticking.

Preparation for the Flam.

lR lR lR lR
* rL rL rL rL

Preparation for Flam Accent No. 1

R   L   R

Preparation for Flam Paradiddle.

L R L L

Preparation for Flamacue

R   L   R   L   R

Write counting under each measure.

EL. 1063

LESSON 26

RUDIMENT REVIEW.

1. Long Roll   2. 5–Stroke Roll   3. 7–Stroke Roll   4. 9–Stroke Roll   5. 13–Stroke Roll

6. Flam   7. Flam Accent No. 1   8. Paradiddle   Flam 9. Paradiddle   10. Flamacue

11. Ruff   12. Single Drag   13. Double Drag   14. Double Paradiddle

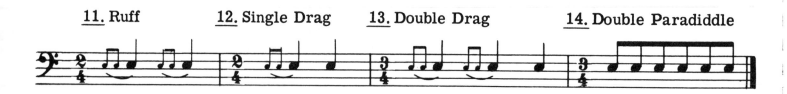

Match the above numbers with the Rudiments listed below.   The first one is done for you.

Test Number 1

Write 10 measures of 4 4 time using notes and rests.   No two measures are to be alike. Write the count under the notes and rests, using x for the rests.

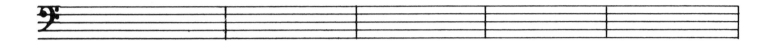

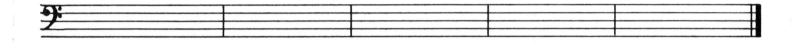

Test Number 2

Write 10 measures of 2 4 time using notes and rests.   No two measures are to be alike. Write the count under the notes and rests, using x for the rests.

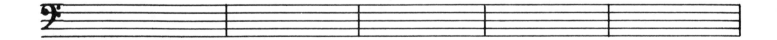

Test Number 3

Write 10 measures of 3 4 time using notes and rests.   No two measures are to be alike.
Write the count under the notes and rests, using x for the rests.

Test Number 4

Write 10 measures of 6 8 time using notes and rests.   No two measures are to be alike.
Write the count under the notes and rests, using x for the rests.

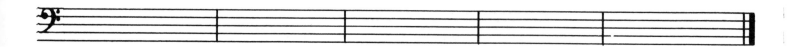

Test Number 5

RUDIMENT RECOGNITION

Match the Rudiment with its respective name.   The first one is done for you.

1.   The Long Roll   [10]

2.   The 5-Stroke Roll   □

3.   The 7-Stroke Roll   □

4.   The 9-Stroke Roll   □

5.   The 13-Stroke Roll   □

6.   The Flam   □

7.   The Flam Accent No. 1   □

8.   The Paradiddle   □

9.   The Flam Paradiddle   □

10.   The Flamacue   □

11.   The Ruff   □

12.   The Single Drag   □

13.   The Double Drag   □

14.   The Double Paradiddle   □

Glossary

1. ≡ staff.

2. 𝄞 - treble clef sign.

3. 𝄢 - bass clef sign.

4. 4/4 - time signature.

5. bar.

6. double bar.

7. measure.

8. ♭ - flat - lowers a note a 1/2 step.

9. ♯ - sharp - raises a note 1/2 step.

10. ♮ - natural - cancels a sharp or flat.

11. leger lines.

12. tie.

13. slur.

14. C - common time. (Same as 4/4 time)

15. repeat section between two sets of dots.

16. D.C. - Da Capo - go back to beginning.

17. D.S. - Del Segna - go back to sign (𝄋).

18. Fine - finish - the end.

19. ⌢ - hold or fermata - give extra time.

20. ⁒ - repeat preceding measure.

21. 1st and 2nd endings. Play 1st ending the first time - then repeat strain and play 2nd ending the second time.

22. ⊕ - coda sign - go to coda.

23. 𝄋 - sign.

24. Key Signature - Flats or sharps placed at the beginning of each line to indicate certain notes that are to be sharped or flatted.

25. *pp* - pianissimo - very soft.

26. *p* - piano - soft.

27. *mp* - mezzo piano - moderately soft.

28. *mf* - mezzo forte - moderately loud.

29. *f* - forte - loud.

30. *ff* - fortissimo - very loud.

31. ◁ - increase volume.

32. ▷ - decrease volume.

33. rit. - ritard - gradually slower.

34. rall. - rallentando - gradually slower.

35. accel. - acqelerando - gradually faster.

36. cresc. - crescendo - gradually louder.

37. dim. - diminuendo - gradually softer.

38. Chromatic scale - a scale that progresses by half steps.

39. ¢ - alla breve, or cut time.

40. ▸ - accent mark - play with force.

41. simile - continue in similar manner.

42. ♩ - staccato - short and repeated.

43. ♪♪♪ - triplets - three notes played in the time of two.